Brain Graft

Laura Solomon

Proverse Hong Kong

2017

BRAIN GRAFT centres around Isobella, who works at a publishing firm and is diagnosed with a brain tumour. She finds a surgeon to remove her tumour and decides to have a brain implant – that is, a segment of brain to fill the space in her brain created by the tumour removal. The segment is donated by another woman, Tracey.

After the transplant, Isobella begins to take on characteristics of Tracey's personality. Isobella's boyfriend, Tarquin, is horrified by this. Isobella begins a slow but steady slide down the socio-economic ladder, losing her job and sitting around the flat all day. Tracey's trajectory is the opposite. She takes a job cleaning at a hospital, where she meets David, a nurse, who encourages her to study for a nursing diploma.

Tracey lands a job as a nurse at a psychiatric hospital, which is where, in the final scene, she crosses paths with Isobella who has been dumped there by an exasperated Tarquin. David has, by this time, dumped Tracey, claiming that he loved her only because he was seeing the world through rose-tinted spectacles due to the anti-depressants he was on. The two women decide to become lesbian lovers.

LAURA SOLOMON has written two previous plays, 'The Dummy Bride' was produced as part of the Wellington Fringe Festival in 1996 and 'Sprout' was performed as part of the Edinburgh Fringe Festival in 2005. Solomon writes, "I was interested in the topic of a brain graft because I was myself diagnosed with a brain tumour."

Solomon is also a prize-winning poet and writer of young adult fiction. *Instant Messages*, her young adult novella, won the inaugural Proverse Prize for unpublished fiction, non-fiction or poetry in 2009. Among her other works published by Proverse are the poetry collections, *In Vitro* and *Frida Kahlo's Cry*, the short story collection, *The Shingle Bar Sea Monster and other stories*, and the novel, *An Imitation of Life*.

# BRAIN GRAFT

*a play by*

# Laura Solomon

*If you can't trust your own brain, then what can you trust?*

**Proverse Hong Kong**

Brain Graft
by Laura Solomon
Copyright © Laura Solomon March 2017
First published in Hong Kong by Proverse Hong Kong,
under sole and exclusive right and license, March 2017.
ISBN: 978-988-8228-64-5

Distribution (Hong Kong and worldwide):
The Chinese University Press of Hong Kong,
The Chinese University of Hong Kong,
Shatin, New Territories, Hong Kong SAR.
Email: cup-bus@cuhk.edu.hk; Web: www.chineseupress.com

Distribution (United Kingdom):
Christine Penney, Stratford-upon-Avon, Warwickshire CV37 6DN, UK.
Email: chrisp@proversepublishing.com

Also available from https://www.createspace.com/6983422

Distribution, performance, and other enquiries to:
Proverse Hong Kong, P.O. Box 259, Tung Chung Post Office,
Tung Chung, Lantau Island, NT, Hong Kong SAR, China.
Email: proverse@netvigator.com; Web: www.proversepublishing.com

The right of Laura Solomon to be identified as the author of this work
has been asserted by her
in accordance with the Copyright, Designs and Patents Act 1988.

Page design, Proverse Hong Kong.
Cover design, Pin-Key Design Co., Hong Kong.

All rights reserved.
No part of this publication may be reproduced, stored in a retrieval system, or transmitted, in any form or by any means, electronic, mechanical, photocopying, recording or otherwise, without the prior written permission of the publisher. The book is sold subject to the condition that it shall not, by way of trade or otherwise, be lent, re-sold, hired out or otherwise circulated without the publisher's prior written consent in any form of binding or cover other than that in which it is published and without a similar condition including this condition being imposed on the subsequent owner or purchaser. Please contact Proverse Hong Kong in writing, to request any and all permissions (including but not restricted to republishing, inclusion in anthologies, translation, reading, performance and use as set pieces in examinations and festivals).

British Library Cataloguing in Publication Data.
A catalogue record for this book is available
from the British Library.

# LIST OF CHARACTERS
(In Order of Appearance)

TARQUIN: Isobella's boyfriend. Hedge fund manager. Early thirties. His life so far has been charmed, nothing bad has ever happened to him.

ISOBELLA: Upper class. Editorial assistant at respectable publishing house. Late twenties.

ISOBELLA'S BOSS: Forties. Firm but fair. Takes care of staff but expects certain standards as she has to keep writers and shareholders happy.

PHYSICIAN: Can be male or female. Polite and professional, but caring rather than cold and clinical.

TRACEY: Working class. Sixteen. Lives in a council estate. Tracey gets a job cleaning at a hospital, then later qualifies and becomes a mental health nurse.

KYLIE: Tracey's best friend. Eighteen. Working class, manages a bar. Lives in same estate as Tracey. She can see the good in Tracey and doesn't want her to go down the same path as Tracey's mother.

ADMIRER

ABORTIONIST

MISCELLANEOUS MAN

DAVID: Tracey's boyfriend whom she meets while cleaning at nursing college.

# AUTHOR'S NOTES TO ACTORS AND DIRECTOR

Tracey should appear very hardened for her sixteen years because of the way she's been treated by society. She should be naturally intelligent, but was born into a bad family, so not given many chances in life. Born with a plastic spoon.

Before surgery Tracey is a bit scatty/naive – she dreams of an easy way out of her harsh situation, so sells her brain segment. After surgery, she has a baby, settles down, becomes more responsible, forgets about dreams – dreams never materialise anyway – and gets a job as a cleaner, something practical she can do.

In contrast, Isobella has had a very privileged life. Born with a silver spoon. Before the tumour, she has never had anything bad happen to her. In many ways she is more fragile than Tracey. Tracey has become hardened through experience. Isobella has led a very sheltered life. Protected by her parents' money. She is a kind person at heart.

Tracey moves up the class system through sheer hard work. Isobella slides down the social scale, mostly because of the tumour/implant. In the end, the two women meet in the middle – in a psychiatric hospital.

Throughout the first few scenes, until the diagnosis of the tumour, Isobella is quite bewildered. After the diagnosis, she is prescribed Dilantin and the seizures she had been having stop.

Time in the play does not always pass at the same rate. The play takes place over the course of five years.

An optional method to signify the passing of time is the use of a projection screen at the rear of the stage. Throughout, this is referred to as The Screen. A portion of The Screen should be allocated to show Date: Time. This should be a digital clock, helping to denote that the play is set in the near future. This should change with each scene to show accurately the Date:

Time. Remains displayed throughout the scene. The rest of The Screen changes to reflect the setting.

## SETS

There are twenty-six scenes and three main settings. The scenes are quite short, and the sets do not have to be moved on/off stage. All sets can be onstage at once and the actors can simply move between sets.

**Bar** – a bar and two barstools. This is variously a dingy bar, and a posh bar. This could be indicated by the use of a prop such as pool cues for the dingy bar or a vase of flowers for posh.

**Office** – desk and two chairs. This is variously a publisher's office, a physician's office, an abortion clinic, and The Centre for Brain Repair. The set may be indicated by different props, for instance, books for the publisher, skeleton figurine on the desk for the physician, a 'woman's choice' poster for the abortion clinic, the Centre for Brain Repair by a chart showing the brain.

**Hospital/Apartment** – two beds. For the apartment scenes, a throw and cushions on the beds could be used to indicate sofas. The hospital set is variously a posh private hospital, a psychiatric hospital, and The Centre for Brain Repair. The apartment set is both Isobella and Tarquin's apartment, and David's apartment.

Sets may be indicated by images projected onto The Screen.

~~~

# SCENE ONE

*The Screen reads 5 February 2030 at 17:37:42.*

*Posh bar.*

*Tarquin is sitting at the bar, toying with a rose. Isobella enters, looking flustered. Tarquin taps the face of his watch.*

**Isobella** Oh gosh, darling. Sorry I'm late. I don't know what's wrong with me – I've just not been myself lately.

**Tarquin** I've noticed. This is the third date in a row you've been late for. I'm finding it all very trying. *(Loudly, showing off, so all the bar can hear.)* You know I've just moved to a more senior position at Take Your Money Fund Management. I'm managing several teams now and this tardiness absolutely *must* be nipped in the bud. On top of my extremely heavy workload, I've got to get all the lads to the country lodge for the pheasant shooting this weekend.

**Isobella** I *am* sorry. It's very out of character. You know I value punctuality above all else. I left work at the right time, but I couldn't seem to navigate my way through the public transport system. I'm actually beginning to get quite worried. There's something not quite right upstairs. *(Taps side of head.)*

*During the following speech, Isobella sits silently, looking unwell.*

**Tarquin** Oh hogwash. There's nothing wrong with your noggin. You've got a First in English Literature from a good university and you're holding down a damned good job as an assistant editor at a top publishing house. It's psychological. Probably just hormones. What you need is a decent rest. A good spot of pheasant shooting will sort you out. Why don't you accompany me and the lads to the country? You'll be waited on hand and foot. The domestic staff are excellent. Besides, Mummy will be there. You two have always got along swimmingly. Remember that spell you went through in your second year of uni? Pushing yourself too hard. You weren't getting enough food and sleep. We went away skiing in Austria for two weeks and you were as right as rain. You don't *always* have to be Number One at everything. And, let's face it, if you weren't so bloody stubborn and accepted my marriage proposal, you'd never have to work again. I know what'll cheer you up. *(Snaps fingers for bartender who doesn't appear.)* A bottle of the Dom Perignon White Gold Jeroboam that you like. By the way, darling, I've taken the liberty of ordering for you, since you were running late. The herb roasted sea bream with lemon and caper dressing.

*Isobella clings onto edge of bar.*

**Isobella** Oh, I don't....feel...don't feel so...g-g-g...

*She falls to floor. Twitches. Tarquin rushes to her side, checks her pulse.*

**Tarquin** Is there a doctor in the house? Somebody call a doctor. Don't just stand around gawking. Can't you see the lady's unwell? Where's a bartender, we need a glass of water.


**SCENE TWO**

*The Screen reads 8 February 2030 at 09:34:09.*

*Publisher's office.*

*Isobella enters, looking confused. Walks to her desk. Types a bit. Puts head in hands. Types a bit more. Puts head in hands. Boss walks over to Isobella's desk.*

**Boss** Late again, Isobella? I'd like to see you in my office please?

*Isobella looks frightened and vulnerable, like a mouse that's about to be eaten by a cat.*

**Boss** Just a quick word. I couldn't help but notice that today's the second day in a row that you've been late. Your work is normally exceptional, but standards have been slipping. We all have our off days, but this has been going on for quite some time now. How's your work/life balance? Is there anything you need to talk to me about?

**Isobella** I don't think so ... my workload's fine, and I've just had a weekend with Tarquin in the country. To be perfectly honest, I'm struggling but I don't know why.

**Boss** We need to get to the bottom of this. I have every faith in your capabilities, but lately you seem to have lost your spark. This publishing house has its reputation to protect. You'll be no good to me today. Go home, take a duvet day – whatever it is you need – but come back to me tomorrow firing on all four cylinders.

**Isobella** Oh look. I *am* sorry. It's never been my intent...inten...int-t-t...to let you...d-d-down...

*Collapses sideways in chair.*

**Boss** Isobella? Are you all right? ...Somebody call an ambulance.


### SCENE THREE

*The Screen reads 15 February 2030 at 11:22:35.*

*Psychiatric hospital.*

*Isobella in bed reading a literary novel. Enter Tarquin carrying a bunch of red roses. Gives her a peck on the mouth.*

**Tarquin** Right then, my little patient. It's been three days, any news yet?

**Isobella** The doctor says it's stress-induced psychosis and manic depression.

**Tarquin** My goodness. That sounds nasty. How do you cure that? Broken bones are easy, but where do you start with a broken mind?

**Isobella** They've offered me ECT, but I turned it down. You know they put me on something called Respirodal. I'm already stacking on the pounds. I'm so worried, Tarquin.

**Tarquin** It's all right. We've just been thrown a bit of a curve ball. We'll sort things out. Great Aunt Fanny went a bit funny in the head for a spell, but she was right as rain in the end. She went on to become Women's Croquet Champion. Some of my great artistic heroes have been bipolar or depressive. Spike Milligan, Steven Fry, what about Churchill? He used to get doses of the old 'black dog'. And how about Morrissey? He's not exactly a cheerful chappie, now is he?

**Isobella** Virginia Woolf, Sylvia Plath, Nina Simone. I'm in good company. My goodness, half the celebs in London have been in this place. It's not so bad in here. Quite nice, actually. They've even got equine assisted therapy.

**Tarquin** Ouch. That sounds painful.

**Isobella** I haven't tried it yet, but Charlotte in the room next door's given it a go and she says it's the greatest thing ever.

**Tarquin** (*Full of himself, but also trying to reassure both himself and Isobella that they can cope. He should have a slight note of panic/hysteria in his voice.*) Oh, a bout of mental illness is nothing to be ashamed of. Every man and his dog has a breakdown these days. It's *de rigueur*, darling. I read in the paper yesterday that the UK is in the grip of a long-term sickness epidemic, which costs businesses an estimated £3.1 billion a year.

**Isobella** £3.1 billion!

*Laura Solomon, Brain Graft*

**Tarquin** So you're not alone in breaking down. Workers are dropping like flies. A third of my colleagues are off sick on stress leave.

**Isobella** The city's just become too fast-paced. People can't hack it. Technology is evolving at ever-increasing speeds. It's all fast, fast, fast. What happened to slow? What happened to down-time? What happened to chilling out? Even yoga's turned into 'power yoga'.

**Tarquin** We're in the grip of a global epidemic of depression.

*Long pause. Isobella looks somewhat stunned. Although she doesn't know it yet, she's also been having seizures, which are leaving her tired and confused.*

**Tarquin** *(giving Isobella a hearty slap on the shoulder)* So rest assured, darling, you're not alone. You'll pull through, old thing. And I'll take care of the fees for this place. You don't have to worry about a thing.

*Gives Isobella a peck on the cheek and exits.*


### SCENE FOUR

*The Screen reads 17 February 2030 at 09:50:55.*

*Physician's Office.*

*Isobella and Physician, seated. Throughout, Isobella has trouble speaking and experiences absence seizures.*

**Physician** Isobella, I've just been reading your files. Nice to put a face to a name.

**Isobella** Nice to meet you, doctor...

**Physician** Please just call me Mark. Now, how have you been?

**Isobella** I'm not getting any better. If anything, I'm getting worse.

**Physician** That must be frustrating. Because you've been quite high-functioning, haven't you? Can you give me some examples of your current problems?

**Isobella** Well, the other day Tarquin came to visit me at the hospital and I wasn't in my room. He was very cross with me. Apparently he'd called me the previous day to arrange a visit and I had absolutely no recollection of the phone call.

**Physician** That *is* unusual. Perhaps we should test your short term memory.

**Isobella** (*stops and stares for about 20 seconds*) Okay.

**Physician** I will read out a list of words on a shopping list and I would like you to repeat them back after me. Eggs, flour, milk, cheese, butter, bread, coffee, tea, sugar, rice.

**Isobella** Milk (*pause*), coffee (*pause*), rice...

**Physician** Not good. What about if I ask you to memorise items from this list?

*Puts list in front of her. Isobella tries to memorise.*

**Isobella** Beans (*pause*), lemons (*pause*), peas... you see?

**Physician** Yes, I see what you mean.

**Isobella** I also seem to be having trouble processing speech. I can't quite understand what people are saying to me. (*Stops and stares for about 20 seconds.*) I-I just don't think that the diagnosis of manic depression is correct.
**Physician** Why not?

**Isobella** Because I'm not manic or depressed.

*Physician scribbles on paper.*

**Isobella** There are also these...fits. I fall to the floor...and afterwards the world is...gelatinous. I struggle to work out how to get from one room to another. It's almost as if I'm intermittently possessed by demons. (*Stops and stares for about 20 seconds.*) My spirit's not quite connected to my body properly. I feel...dislocated.

**Physician** I know we've diagnosed this as psychological, but we shouldn't dismiss the notion that it could be a neurological condition. Let's book you in for a CAT scan. If it shows an abnormality, we'll need an MRI to determine exactly what it is that we're dealing with. We should book you in for an EEG as well. To see if you're having seizures.

**Isobella** What's an EEG?

**Physician** They attach electrodes to your head to monitor electrical activity in the brain.

**Isobella** Okay, as long as there are no harmful side effects. It's not like ECT is it?

**Physician** Oh no, no. Completely safe.

**Isobella** All right then. That sounds fine.

**Physician** Good, I'll get you booked in.

**Isobella** (*stops and stares for about 20 seconds*) Thanks.

**Physician** You're welcome.

## SCENE FIVE

*The Screen reads 20 February 2030 at 10:42:40.*

*Physician's Office.*

*Physician is seated in a chair. Enter Isobella.*

**Physician** Oh hello Isobella. Last week's CAT scan showed an abnormality. You then had your MRI and I've now got the results back.

**Isobella** *(bracing self, gripping edge of chair)* What's the verdict?

**Physician** The abnormality that we saw on the CAT scan is definitely a tumour – a grade two astrocytoma. These 'fits' you are speaking of will be seizures.

**Isobella** I knew it wasn't manic depression! I absolutely knew there must be something more wrong. How long has it been there for? How long have I got left to live?

**Physician** It looks like you've probably had it for years. Perhaps since you were a girl. You'll have to see a neurologist to find out how long you have left to live.

**Isobella** So all this time I've had a tumour slowly eating my brain?

**Physician** Causing small seizures at first. Little earthquakes. Petit mals. Then there was the grand mal seizure you told me about. You can die during a seizure, did you know that?

**Isobella** Yes, I felt my spirit leave my body.

**Physician** In rare cases, if the seizure goes on for too long, the brain can starve of oxygen.

**Isobella** Where do we take it from here then?

**Physician** Surgery's your best bet. Do you have private health insurance?

**Isobella** Um, I'm not sure.

**Physician** If not, you'll have to go on the NHS waiting list.

**Isobella** Don't like the sound of that much.

**Physician** No. Nobody does. We've also got the results of your EEG back.

**Isobella** What are the results?

**Physician** Nothing out of the ordinary in your brainwaves. But that doesn't mean you're not having absence seizures. Not all types of seizure are picked up on an EEG. Some are so deep in the brain that they won't register. We should also try you on Dilantin for the seizures. Even these spells where you're having trouble talking could be absence seizures.

**Isobella** What's an absence seizure?

**Physician** Call it a momentary loss of awareness. In your case, you just *stop* for twenty seconds or so. A momentary lapse of reason.

**Isobella** Oh God, do you have to quote Pink Floyd at a time like this?
*Physician scribbles.*

**Physician** Here's the script. You can take it to any pharmacy.

**Isobella** Great, thanks.

**Physician** You're welcome.

## SCENE SIX

*The Screen reads 20 February 2030 at 21:32:35.*

*Dingy bar.*

*Tracey is getting drunk at the bar. Singing 'Walk This Way' really badly on karaoke. Attracts the attention of Admirer. Ends up snogging Admirer. Kylie watches in dismay. Tracey has quick knee-trembler up against a wall. Admirer runs off.*


## SCENE SEVEN

*The Screen reads 18 April 2030 at 18:50:55.*

*Dingy bar.*

*Kylie behind bar, serving drinks. Enter Tracey, exhausted. Slumps down on bar stool. Throughout the following sequence, Tracey gets more and more irate and Kylie gets more and more preachy.*

**Kylie** The usual?

**Tracey** Yeah. Make it a double, since you've just been promoted to manager of this place and I'm drowning my sorrows.

**Kylie** What's eating you then?

*Tracey whips out a pregnancy tester.*

**Kylie** Oh God, Trace. You're not up the duff again, are you? You'll end up like your bloody mother. Looking for the answer at the bottom of a bottle of gin. Mother's little helper. She told you she didn't want to be a grandmother before forty.

**Tracey** All right, all right, don't bang on. At least I'm not in tears. I used to cry when I was younger, but where did that ever get me? Nobody gives a shit about a sob. Better to have a tequila and forget about it. Cripes, the world is full of losers. Why'd I have to get up the duff to one? All I want is a good man to take me out to Nandoes and buy me half a chicken.

**Kylie** That's probably what your mum once wanted too. Now she's got three kids to support. Three different fathers, three different colours. Two of the fathers are in clink, including your Dad. Grand theft auto, wasn't it?

**Tracey** Yeah, like the game, but in real life. Only knew his own kid for six months before they put him inside.

**Kylie** Who's the lucky bloke then? What's his last name?

**Tracey** Last name? Don't even know his first name, do I? It was just a one night stand. A split condom. You remember, karaoke night two months ago? Right, girlfriend – come with me to the abortion clinic. Same as last time.

**Kylie** You can't have another abortion, Trace.

**Tracey** Why not?

**Kylie** Because it's murder. You're killing a person.

**Tracey** *(defensively)* It's *my* body. Anyway, a collection of human cells isn't necessarily a person. I've already had one abortion, what does a second one matter? Easy come, easy go.

**Kylie** Human life begins at conception. Killing a human is wrong, therefore, abortion is wrong.

**Tracey** *(sarcastically)* Whatever. Been looking at pro-life websites, have ya?
**Kylie** Destroying a foetus is destroying a human's future.

**Tracey** *(getting more irate)* What about *my* future? What about *my fucking future?* I know it's not exactly rosy living on a council estate, but Cripes, I'm only sixteen. I can hardly even look after meself, let alone a baby. What kind of Britain is this to bring a sprog into anyway? Rising unemployment, massive recession, racism, sexism, mugging, looting, riots, random acts of violence. Not exactly peachy is it?

**Kylie** Destroying a foetus is destroying a human life.

**Tracey** Surely the foetus is better off dead then it is growing up with a mother who's too young to take care of it.

**Kylie** What about the rights of the baby?

**Tracey** What about *my* rights? Women's right to choose and all that. The right to make decisions. You're so anti-abortion; but what about in the case of the woman who's been raped? *(Pause)* You'll come with me to the clinic, won't you Kylie?

**Kylie** Oh God. Do I have to? I hate that place. It's creepy as hell.

**Tracey** Who else is going to come with me? It's not as if I have any other decent friends to rely on. Amanda and them are partying all summer. Fair weather friends them lot are. It's you I can rely on Kylie – you're my solid rock.

**Kylie** You need to get parental consent.

**Tracey** Mum's consented. I asked her last night. She was half sloshed at the time, but then that's nothing new.

**Kylie** All right then. The abortion clinic it is.

**Tracey** I've made the appointment for ten tomorrow morning. We'll take the bus. I'll swing by yours to pick you up.

## SCENE EIGHT

*The Screen reads 19 April 2030 at 09:45:01.*

*Office. Abortion clinic.*

*Tracey and Kylie in a working class suburb. A group of pro-lifers hanging around, with placards upon which are written the following slogans: Abortion Kills a Beating Heart, God Hates Abortion, Everyone Should Have a Birthday, Ban Stem Cell Research. The pro-lifers are blocking the door. They start pointing and spitting at Tracey and Kylie, yelling 'KILLERS', etc as Tracey and Kylie try to get past. Tracey should be looking vulnerable. Kylie puts her arm protectively around Tracey's shoulders and ushers her through. The Abortionist sits in a chair. Tracey approaches, sits down opposite.*

**Abortionist** Here we are then. Two pills to take. Mifepristone and Prosta-glandin. Take the Mifepristone now. *(Hands over another pill.)* This is Phenergan – for nausea. Here are the Misoprostol suppositories. Use them ten hours after taking the Mifepristone. You will likely begin to experience bleeding, passing of blood clots, and cramping within a few hours of inserting the Misoprostol. Most women will pass the pregnancy from their body within 24 hours of inserting the Misoprostol suppositories. In a small number of cases, it can take weeks for the pregnancy to be expelled. If you see the nurse on reception, she can book you a follow-up exam for three to four weeks after treatment, to ensure that the abortion is complete.

**Tracey** Great, thanks.

*Kylie and Tracey head home.*

## SCENE NINE

*The Screen reads 28 May 2030 at 19:22:35.*

*Dingy bar.*

*Kylie behind bar serving drinks. Enter Tracey. Kylie pours her a double whiskey without having to be asked.*

**Kylie** Did you take them pills then?

**Tracey** Nah man. Wimped out at the last minute. Got all sentimental, didn't I?

**Kylie** What, you? Little Miss Hard-As-Bloody-Nails. I thought all your sentiment flew out the window when you came home to find your next-door-neighbour raping your mother. If that wouldn't toughen up a twelve year old, then what would?

**Tracey** I've made up my mind. I'm keeping my baby.

**Kylie** Oh Cripes. Do you have to quote Madonna at a time like this?

**Tracey** Madonna's a woman of the world, she knows what she's on about. She didn't get to be a millionaire by being stupid, did she?

**Kylie** Are you sure this is a decision you have thought through properly? Just the other day you were fully into the abortion.

**Tracey** *(defensively)* I *am* allowed to change my mind, aren't I? *(Sarcastically)* That *is* within my human rights, I presume?

**Kylie** You do realise that once you've passed the three month mark they won't give you an abortion?

**Tracey** Of course I realise that; I'm not an idiot.

**Kylie** How are you and the baby gonna survive?

**Tracey** I'll go on the dole and supplement my income with a bit of cleaning work. Anyway, you're a fine one to talk about changing your mind. Just the other day you were fully against the abortion and trying to talk me into keeping the baby. Now you've done a one-eighty, what gives? You getting a kick out of playing devil's advocate or something?

**Kylie** I'm just making sure that you've thought through all the ins and outs. A baby's not just for Christmas.

**Tracey** Who made you my surrogate mother?

*Long pause, implying that that is exactly what Kylie is to Tracey. Kylie hands Tracey a pen and paper.*

**Kylie** Right. Make me a list of pros and cons. Get it down on a piece of paper. That always helps me to think more clearly.

**Tracey** You've been reading too many self-help books.

**Kylie** Better than developing an addiction to daytime soaps, like you!

**Tracey** (*sniggers*) All right then, boss. A list it is. *(Starts making list.)*

PROS for keeping baby: Never alone. Somebody to visit me in the retirement home possibly. (*Sarcastically*) The rosy joys of motherhood. I've already murdered one baby and I don't want it to be habit-forming – I don't want to become a serial baby-killer. We live in the UK, not Russia, where abortion is a form of contraception.

CONS against keeping baby: Never alone, never any time for myself. Smelly nappies. Vomit. Expensive.

**Kylie** Right, let's add it up. Five pros and four cons. Madonna wins. You're keeping the baby.

**Tracey** *(Pushes whiskey glass towards Kylie.)* Come on then. Pour us another one.

**Kylie** Not if you're keeping the sprog. *(Takes fag from Tracey's lips.)* No smoking either.

**Tracey** Crikey, Mum!

**Kylie** There's two of you to think about now.

**Tracey** *(rolls her eyes)* And other bloody clichés.

**Kylie** So how are you going to support yourself with a kid?

**Tracey** There's nothing for it Kylie, I'm going to have to go on the game.

**Kylie** Don't get into hooking Tracey. It's a downward spiral. You'll pick up all kinds of diseases. Sleep with a dog you get fleas.

**Tracey** It'll be all right. Just use condoms. It could be like that film – *Pretty Woman*. Might find myself a rich sugar daddy.

**Kylie** Crikey, Trace. Be realistic. You'll end up having to sleep with fat, hairy men with huge beer guts. I won't let you do it. Listen – I have a much better plan.

*Whips out a tabloid magazine from under the counter.*

**Kylie** Says here about selling body parts. The money's not bad.

**Tracey** What, like in that movie *Dirty Pretty Things*? I saw that just last week, I did.

**Kylie** *(enthusiastically)* Five hundred quid for a little toe. Two grand for a kidney. Five grand for a brain segment.

**Tracey** Five thousand quid! That'd go a long way towards supporting the kid.

**Kylie** You can go to this Centre for Brain Repair to find out all about it.

**Tracey** Can I really sell a section of brain?

**Kylie** Why not? Plenty of other people are doing it. It says they've already had twenty volunteers.

**Tracey** (*pause*) I'll think about it, okay. After all, they say that humans only use ten percent of our brain anyway. And five thousand quid is five thousand quid.

### SCENE TEN

*The Screen reads 15 June 2030 at 09:15:48.*

*Office. The Centre for Brain Repair.*

*Enter Isobella.*

**Physician** Oh hello.

**Isobella** Hello, I'm Isobella.

**Physician** I know. I've been expecting you.

**Isobella** I've come to see you about brain surgery. I was wondering what you would advise? Risks versus benefits.

**Physician** The risks are death during surgery. Infection after removing a section of the cranium. You could have a stroke during surgery. And with the location of your tumour, your right leg could be affected and you could walk with a slight limp.

**Isobella** Oh. What are the benefits?

**Physician** Controlling the tumour. Currently it's only grade two – benign. This could progress to a higher grade; it could turn malignant.

**Isobella** I don't much like the sound of that.

**Physician** No sane person would. *(Pause)* There's also a new discovery I've been wanting to share with you. The possibility of a brain implant. Of course you would need to take immunosuppressant drugs to stop your body rejecting the graft.

**Isobella** That sounds adventurous. Sort of like a breast implant, but different. Brain implant. How does it work?

**Physician** You have surgery side by side with a donor. They donate a section of brain from the same area as your tumour and it gets implanted in your brain.

**Isobella** Sounds like something out of Ishiguro's novel *Never Let Me Go*. I've just finished reading that. Do I get to meet the donor?

**Physician** Sure. We've got a young lady called Tracey lined up. We just need to make sure that her blood type matches yours. She'll be in later today for a blood test. I'll run the concept of meeting you by her.

**Isobella** But what if my brain rejects the implant?

**Physician** They give you anti-rejection drugs. And drugs to suppress your immune system. That reminds me, you should be taking anti-seizure medication. Are you on Dilantin?

**Isobella** Yes, I am. So will I be awake during the operation – an awake craniotomy? I've read about that in *National Geographic*. It stated that the human brain has no nerves; it feels no pain – is that right?

**Physician** Yes, that's correct. However, the tumour's not in a location that requires functional mapping so we won't have to do an awake craniotomy.

**Isobella** I'll have to discuss these issues with my boyfriend.

**Physician** Of course.

## SCENE ELEVEN

*The Screen reads 15 June 2030 at 10:27:39.*

*Office. The Centre for Brain Repair.*

*Doctor sitting in chair.*

**Physician** Hello, you must be Tracey.

**Tracey** That's my name, don't wear it out.

*Doctor grimaces.*

**Tracey** I'm here to sell a chunk of me brain. Have I come to the right place?

**Physician** Yes. That's right.

**Tracey** What's the deal then? What section of me brain do you need? *(Gestures directions with hands.)* Front, back, left, right?

**Physician** We need a section of your left frontal lobe.

**Tracey** What's that responsible for then?

**Physician** Personality.

**Tracey** *(reacting rather than stopping to think)* I can't sell you a section of my personality!! That'd be like selling you a section of my soul.

**Physician** Well, that's the section we need. That's the part that is being removed from the donee's brain, so that's the part you have to donate.

**Tracey** *(stops to think, calculates)* All right then. But not for five grand. Five grand'd be reasonable if it was hand movement or something I was selling. But personality's extra, man, personality's *me! (Going in aggressive.)* Ten grand for personality. Ten grand and you got yourself a deal.

**Physician** I'll have to check with the client. She's the one who's paying. Let me see if our receptionist can get her on the phone.

**Tracey** Okay. Check and get back to me.

*Physician exits. Two minute pause.*

**Physician** The client's come back with seven and a half grand.

**Tracey** Oh, like that is it. Haggling over the price.

**Physician** What do you think?

**Tracey** Okay. Seven and a half grand it is. Do I get to meet her then? This 'client'. What's her name anyway?

**Physician** Isobella.

**Tracey** *Isobella, Oh,* I say! One of them posh ladies is she? All hoighty toighty and up her own arse and what not.

*Pause. Deliberate no comment from doctor.*

**Tracey** Come on then. When do I get to meet her?

**Physician** Speak to the receptionist and she'll arrange a meeting.

## SCENE TWELVE

*The Screen reads 15 June 2030 at 19:45:40.*

*Posh bar.*

**Tarquin** How did it go at The Centre for Brain Repair?

**Isobella** Well, I want to have the operation. It sounds like it's best to have surgery for this type of tumour. However, I have my doubts about surgery. I mean, why should I trust a medical professional after all that I've been through so far? I felt like Spike Milligan with his 'told you I was ill', only in my case it was more like 'told you I was confused'. They misdiagnosed me as having manic depression when I had a brain tumour. Why did nobody think to scan my brain earlier? Now they want to poke around inside my skull. Why should I let a surgeon invade my brain? I've lost all faith in the medical profession.

**Tarquin** Oh come on, sweetheart. You know that doctors are only human. They're all over-worked. They're humans, not robots and humans make mistakes. Even robots make mistakes. You've got to have faith.

**Isobella** Oh God, do you have to quote George Michael at a time like this? Besides, remember that Harley Street acupuncturist I went to. He harassed me.

**Tarquin** No, I don't recall. In what way?

**Isobella** I told him I was into the arts and he asked me if I was a perceptive sort of a person. When I replied that I was he asked me would I feel it if a horny man was standing behind me, staring at the back of my head.

**Tarquin** Disgusting. I agree. That sort of thing's not on in this day and age.

**Isobella** Sexual harassment is rarely about sex.

**Tarquin** What is it about then?

**Isobella** Power and control. Men trying to make women feel vulnerable and intimidated so that they can feel better about themselves. Especially women they feel threatened by.

*Lengthy pause, as Tarquin digests this.*

**Tarquin** At any rate, leave it to me. I'll check with Uncle Arthur – he's retired now, but he used to be a doctor. He'll have friends in the know. We won't send you to any old quack, contacts darling, connections. We'll send you to the crème de la crème of brain surgeons, only the best for you. Leave this business to me.

**Isobella** Business? Why does everything have to be business these days? This isn't one of your mergers you're orchestrating. This is my life. The life of a human being. I've been on and off every med, allergic to half, gained three kilos, and misdiagnosed as manic depressive. I feel like I've lost the reins to my life. They must be in somebody else's hands, because they're not in mine. So, they may as well be in your hands, Tarquin. Listen, the best thing is for me to hand control and responsibility over to you. I know that I'm a feminist but in this case it really is better to hand things over to the man. We've been together for five years now. I really trust you and I know that you'll do the right thing.

**Tarquin** I wholeheartedly agree, sweetheart. I know it's been over 50 years since 'Suffragette City' and women have had the vote for many years, but gentlemen are gents and ladies are ladies. When we are faced with a problem of this magnitude – I consider it my manly duty to protect you from further harm. Leave it to me, you know you're in safe hands.

**Isobella** There's also this new thing the physician discussed with me. Never heard of it before. It's called a brain implant.

**Tarquin** Gosh, that sounds exciting. How does that work?

**Isobella** Well, they find a donor whose blood type matches yours. They take a segment of that person's brain and implant it. I'll be meeting the donor in a couple of weeks.

**Tarquin** I'll help in any way I can. You know I want to help.

**Isobella** Would you really?

**Tarquin** Of course. You know I want to fix you.

**Isobella** Oh God, do you have to quote Coldplay at a time like this?

*They clink glasses and exchange a kiss.*


## SCENE THIRTEEN

*The Screen reads 1 July 2030 at 11:35:20.*

*Office. The Centre for Brain Repair.*

*Tracey is young and naïve. Shows a frightening lack of concern about a major operation. Isobella is nervous and more fragile.*

**Isobella** (*extends hand*) Oh hello, I'm Isobella.

**Tracey** Tracey's me name. So it's you who's going to be getting a lump of me brain, is it?

**Isobella** Yes, if it all goes according to plan. It's rather nerve-racking, isn't it? (*Gesturing to Tracey's stomach.*) I see you're pregnant. Aren't you rather worried about undergoing such a major operation while with child?

**Tracey** Na, mate, kushdie. They did tests on me and the baby this morning. Whole lot of checks. Blood pressure, heart rate. They even did one of them EEG thingies, you know with the strange white suckers on the head and the burny paste. My bloomin' head was on fire.

**Isobella** By 'white suckers' I assume you mean electrodes.

**Tracey** Yeah, that'll be them.

**Isobella** So, tell me a bit about yourself. What do you do for a living?

**Tracey** On the dole. That's why I'm here, innit? Get a chunk of cash. Easy money. Saves going on the game. You were 'raised', weren't ya? Probably went to a finishing school in Switzerland, didn't ya? I was *dragged* up, me. I was more of a mother to my mother than she was a mother to me. Didn't have a bloody childhood, did I? Too busy making sure that Mum was okay. Oh, and I'm only up the duff, and all. That's another good reason I need the money.

**Isobella** (*quite taken aback*) Oh…oh…I see. Will you and the baby be all right after the operation?

**Tracey** Don't you worry about me. Graduated from the school of hard knocks, I did. Seven and a half grand's enough to set me and the baby up. Live on the smell of an oily rag, me. *(Winks.)* So, what's your story? Why d'ya need a piece of me brain anyway? What's the matter with ya?

**Isobella** Oh, didn't they tell you?

**Tracey** No, seems to operate on a need-to-know basis round here.

**Isobella** I've been diagnosed with a grade two astrocytoma.

**Tracey** What's that when it's at home?

**Isobella** A brain tumour.

**Tracey** Oh, that's a bit of a bummer. How long you had that then? You look all right to me.

**Isobella** They say it's been there since I was a child.

**Tracey** How come it took them so long to find it then?

**Isobella** Apparently they're rather hard to diagnose. It wasn't until I started having seizures that I became aware of any problem.

**Tracey** *(flippant)* You'll be all right, sweetheart. Our puppy used to have fits. Used to wet himself and all. He grew out of it. Listen, fancy a cup of tea from the vending machine?

**Isobella** *(looks horrified at the suggestion)* I can't, sorry. Must dash. I'm having lunch with my partner at a local Italian place.

**Tracey** Right you are then. See you on the big day, eh?


### SCENE FOURTEEN

*The Screen reads 1 July 2030 at 19:42:24.*

*Posh bar.*

*Isobella sitting at bar, sipping drink. Tarquin comes rushing in, on the phone. Snaps his fingers for a bartender. At this stage, Tarquin and Isobella are convinced that the segment of brain can ascend the class system.*

**Tarquin** What a day. I've been up to my eyeballs in meetings. But enough about me. How was your day, sweetheart?

**Isobella** Good news. It all went swimmingly.

**Tarquin** What went swimmingly?
**Isobella** The meeting with the brain donor.

**Tarquin** Oh darling, with the merger happening it clean went out of my head. So, do fill me in. What's she like, this…donor?

**Isobella** Well…*(pause)* rather common, but that's all there is available. It's awfully tragic, when young girls start selling body parts for money.

**Tarquin** You're too soft for your own good. People like us can't waste our time worrying about life's casualties. She's a commodity, a resource. The real question is, do you really want a segment of a commoner's brain implanted into yours?

**Isobella** Oh Tarquin, you big oaf. It'll be fine. I'll be able to train that part of the brain. I've read a plethora of articles in a neurology journal. The 'segment' will be able to be educated. A pet brain segment.

**Tarquin** Oh, I say. Do you mean like in *Educating Rita?*

**Isobella** Exactly. A *Pygmalion* for the 21$^{st}$ century.

**Tarquin** *(enthused )* Oh what fun. Training a section of brain. Sort of like training a puppy. We can transform the segment from common to posh.

**Isobella** Think of the experiment as our little project. *(Long pause.)* Mind you, what if something goes wrong?

**Tarquin** What could possibly go wrong?

**Isobella** Not sure. But they've only done twenty of these implants. That's not that many.

**Tarquin** You can be a pioneer.

**Isobella** Oh, I like the sound of that.

*Tarquin kisses her on the cheek. They sip their wine confidently, king and queen of their own little world, convinced that they have surmounted the obstacle that life has thrown their way.*

## SCENE FIFTEEN

*The Screen reads 12 September 2030 at 08:42:24.*

*Posh private hospital.*

*Tracey is awake. Isobella's side of the room is full of bouquets of flowers. Tracey's side of the room has none. Tracey fidgets, twists, turns. Pulls at bandages. Looks around at surroundings. Gets pole that levers the window open. Starts poking Isobella with pole. Isobella wakes up confused and disorientated.*

**Isobella** Where am I? What's happening?

**Tracey** It's the morning after.

**Isobella** Morning after what?

**Tracey** The operation, dummy. Have you lost your marbles? How you feeling then?

**Isobella** Perfectly well, thank you. Bit groggy from the anaesthetic, but all in all, not too shabby.

**Tracey** I feel brilliant. Full of beans. I could go clubbing. Cor, this place is posh. I thought I'd be in a shabby old NHS wing.

**Isobella** Tarquin's taken care of everything.

**Tracey** Who's Tarquin?

**Isobella** My boyfriend.

**Tracey** Oh, aren't I lucky? Landed meself a sugar mummy. Sort of like in that movie, *Pretty Woman*. Only this is *Ugly Woman* instead.

**Isobella** Don't be so hard on yourself. You're an attractive young lady. Is there a man on the scene?

**Tracey** No. But there's been several men fleeing the scene.

**Isobella** Like that. is it. Oh well. Somebody special will come along.

**Tracey** Oh, that old cliché – plenty more fish in the sea and all that junk. Doubt it. I'm off men anyway. Maybe I should start trying women.

*Long pause. Isobella looks uncomfortable.*
*Isobella picks up the room service menu.*

**Isobella** Would you like something to eat?

**Tracey** Yeah, I'm starvin'. Could eat a scabby horse.

**Isobella** A scabby horse? How about some eggs benedict?

**Tracey** Benedict, what's that when it's at home? Oh no matter. Eat anything me. Make mine a supersize.


### SCENE SIXTEEN

*The Screen reads 19 October 2030 at 18:15:35.*

*Isobella and Tarquin's apartment.*

*Isobella is sitting on a sofa, reading trashy magazine. Soundtrack of TV. She is wearing a turquoise boob tube, stone-washed jeans and white-tasselled high-heeled boots, squirting processed cheese into her mouth. Enter Tarquin wearing a tuxedo and holding an orchid. Tarquin sees Isobella and drops beside her in dismay.*

**Tarquin** Oh darling, what on earth are you wearing? Didn't you remember we are off to hear the reed quintet tonight at the concert hall?

**Isobella** What's wrong with what I'm wearing?

**Tarquin** Nothing. I'm sure you'll fit right in with all the other people wearing boob tubes and jeans at a concert hall.

*Isobella turns back to her magazine.*

**Tarquin** What's that junk you're reading?

*Snatches magazine from her hands.*

**Tarquin** What rubbish. What's happened to your Margaret Atwood and your Alice Munro?

**Isobella** *(apathetically)* Dunno. Gone out the window, I guess.

**Tarquin** Lame. Put down that bloody processed cheese and get up off the sofa. We've got a concert to attend.

*Takes Isobella's hand and tries to pull her up off the sofa.*

**Tarquin** Get changed into that lovely ballgown your mother bought you last Christmas.

**Isobella** No way. I'm happy with my processed cheese and *Eastenders*.

**Tarquin** I'm losing my girlfriend. We were the toast of the town! The happy couple. Me, descended from a long line of French aristocracy. Given a million pounds on my twenty-first birthday. I can't think what you saw in me.

**Isobella** Ah yes. We met through the theatre. It was after *The History Boys*. I was in the foyer. You sidled up and bought me a glass of Pinot Noir. It all went forwards from there.

**Tarquin** What's happened to my girlfriend of old? The one who loved the theatre, the one who wore Dolce & Gabbana and Jimmy Choo and doused herself in French perfume? You stink like a polecat. Go on, get in the shower, dolly yourself up, put your face on.

**Isobella** Sorry dude, being posh is just too much bloody effort.

*Squirts cheese into mouth.*

**Tarquin** Fine, be like that then. 'Sorry dude' indeed. (*Snorts*) I'll take Christina, she's been popping into work quite a lot lately.

**Isobella** Whatever.

*Isobella squirts cheese into mouth. Tarquin picks up phone.*

**Tarquin** Oh hello Christine. It's Tarquin here. I've got a spare ticket to hear the reed quintet at the concert hall. Would you like to accompany me?

*Isobella cranks up the volume on TV. Tarquin stomps from the room shooting Isobella a filthy look.*


### SCENE SEVENTEEN

*The Screen reads 28 November 2030 at 20:15:35.*

*Dingy bar.*

*Kylie behind bar. Tracey enters, carrying a baby. Kylie pours her drink without having to ask.*

**Kylie** Hey you! Can't you see the sign on the door? No minors?

**Tracey** What you talking about? Oh (*gestures towards baby*), Little Chardonnay here.

**Kylie** Chardonnay? What kind of a name is that?

**Tracey** It's what I was pissed on when I got up the duff, weren't it? Perfect name for a perfect baby. Pure and crystal clear.

*Sips at drink, rather than slugging it back.*

**Tracey** All right mate, now that I've got a baby, it's time to face reality. No more selling of body parts – one segment of brain is enough. It's time to get a job that I can realistically manage. The money from the brain sale's not going to last forever. They say that a girl's got to have dreams, but that's a load of bull. Dreams like those are made of spun sugar and air – they're fantasies, delusions. Candy-floss. A way of denying and escaping real life. Why would I build my life on a foundation of candy-floss? Better to kiss goodbye to dreams and build my life on solid bricks. Start small. A cleaning job at the psychiatric hospital. Saw the ad in the paper. I know it's not glamorous or nothing, but at least it's guaranteed money. Not much, seven quid an hour, but it's better than having pie in the sky hopes that never amount to anything. Let's face it. I've been cleaning up after Mum for ten years anyway. Cleaning up her puke from when she gets drunk and upchucks. A job'll be good for me. I'll be able to meet other people, get out of the house. It'll stop me wallowing.

**Kylie** I like it Trace. You've woken up to reality. What'll you do with the baby though? S'pose the hospital will have a crèche?

**Tracey** Yeah, they have. I checked it out online.

**Kylie** Go for it then. You'll get the job easy. All that experience with your mother. Look good on the CV.

**Tracey** What's a CV?

**Kylie** You don't know what a CV is? Crikey, Trace, get with the real world. Listen, I'll help you write it now. I'll give you a reference for cleaning this place. *(Winks)* Come on, everybody knows you've been cleaning at the bar for years.

**Tracey** Oh, you're a mate and a half, you are.

*Tracey gives Kylie a high five.*


### SCENE EIGHTEEN

*The Screen reads 2 December 2030 at 20:45:52.*

*Dingy bar.*

*Isobella on karaoke singing 'Walk This Way', really, really badly. Comes off karaoke to pitiful, sarcastic smattering of applause. Isobella heads over to pretend pool table.*

**Isobella** All right lads. Rack up them balls.

*Isobella takes shot after shot, missing them all. Swills lager.*

**Miscellaneous Man** Hello love. Not much of a pool shark then, are you?

**Isobella** Not much of a shark at anything. More of a guppy. A tiddler, a tadpole.

**Miscellaneous Man** What you do for a living then?

**Isobella** I get by.

**Miscellaneous Man** Oh, surely you can do better than that.

**Isobella** I used to work in publishing. Then I got brain cancer. They chopped out the tumour and put in a new segment of brain from a donor. I feel like a whole new woman.

**Miscellaneous Man** Wow. You're kidding me.

**Isobella** Best thing is, I'm much happier this way. I don't miss my old life one bit. The snobbery of the publishing industry. The never-ending competitiveness, always having to keep up with the Joneses. Always having to have the right bag, the right shoes. The right 'look'. And always having to say and do the right thing.

**Miscellaneous Man** *(moving in, trying to hit on her)* Oh, that must have been a terrible strain.

**Isobella** My goodness, the *pressure*. Of course, Mummy and Daddy had raised me properly, so it wasn't terribly difficult for me to fit in. Now I'm having a whale of a time. Hanging out in funky suburbs. Drinking my lager and lime, 'chillin' me boots'.

**Tarquin** *(standing at side of stage – posh voice)* I couldn't believe that *Isobella* had abandoned our relationship to hang out in a pool parlour. Her parents called to tell me how she was living, that there were cigarette burns in the sheets and twenty empty booze bottles in the hall. I was *horrified*.

**Miscellaneous Man** *(putting his arm around Isobella's shoulders)* Come on then sweetheart. Give us a snog.

*Isobella hesitates then begins to kiss Miscellaneous Man.*

**Miscellaneous Man** *(creepily – moving in for the kill)* That's my girl.

*Slides hand down Isobella's top or up skirt, or something equally sleazy.*

## SCENE NINETEEN

*The Screen reads 12 December 2030 at 11:45:15.*

*Psychiatric hospital.*

*Tracey cleaning and singing part of the Beyoncé song, 'Single Ladies (Put a Ring on it)', the lines beginning "Pull me into your arms" followed by the chorus, "Cause if you liked it...". (To perform the lyrics will need permission. If not sought and obtained, Tracey can simply hum the song.)*

*Breaks into a Beyoncé-style dance. A sign on the floor reads 'Slippery When Wet'. David enters. Slips over, falls flat on back.*

**Tracey** Hey you! Didn't you see the sign? Slippery when wet.

**David** Oh Goodness, do you have to quote Bon Jovi at a time like this?

*Clocks Tracey. Sees that she is good-looking. Hams up injury to attract her attention.*

**David** *(clutching tailbone)* Ouch...Oh God, my tailbone.

**Tracey** *(falling for it)* Sheesh, are you all right? Here, take my hand.

*She extends her hand, which David takes. Tracey pulls him to his feet.*

**David** Thanks. Gosh. You're a strong young lady.

**Tracey** You one of the nurses?

**David** Yes, I certainly am. *(Extends hand.)* Hi, I'm David. Fancy having a cuppa in the caf?

**Tracey** *(shakes)* I'm Tracey. And sure, I could do with a break.

# SCENE TWENTY

*The Screen reads 8 January 2031 at 15:52:20.*

*Dingy bar.*

**David** I'm all for furthering oneself through education. You don't have to be a cleaning lady forever.

**Tracey** What do you mean? What the hell else am I going to do? It's not as if I have any formal qualifications or anything?

**David** Did you get your GCSEs?

**Tracey** Yeah, I passed everything. I didn't get amazing grades, but I scraped through. Why?

**David** You could do a nursing diploma. Nursing's a good steady career. People will always need nurses.

**Tracey** (*diffident, lacking in confidence*) Oh, I couldn't. I'm not clever enough. Nobody in my family's ever done anything as fancy as a diploma. Anyway, how would I fit it in with my cleaning?

**David** You could do both part-time. Evenings.

*Lengthy pause as Tracey digests this.*

**Tracey** Do you really think it's something I could do?

**David** Yes. And I could support you. Egg you on, encourage you. Your home life doesn't sound like much to write home about. There's heaps of room in my flat. You could move in with me.

**Tracey** Oh, I couldn't ask that of you. Mind you, it'd be great to live in a nice flat. Be much better than Mum's scummy old council estate.

**David** Be much safer for you and the baby. Think about it anyway.

*Hands her a pamphlet.*

**David** I picked up this pamphlet for you. It's got information about the diploma.

**Tracey** Thanks. (*Takes pamphlet.*) I've made up my mind. I'll do the course. Worth a crack, innit. I mean, Darn, I've survived a horrendous upbringing, an abortion and brain surgery all by the age of seventeen. How hard can a goddamned nursing diploma be?

**Tracey** *(direct address)* With my exemplary work ethic, I soon gained my diploma and became one of the best mental health nurses at the hospital. I had the right manner. Polite but professional. I said and did all the right things. It was sort of like acting. I started out by impersonating the other nurses and then it all became rather natural.

### SCENE TWENTY-ONE

*The Screen reads 13 February 2035 at 07:45:15.*

*David's apartment.*

*Tracey and David wake up in bed together. Cot to one side containing four-year old Chardonnay. Cold atmosphere. Up until now David has been a caring bloke. Now he becomes cold and selfish – hardened.*

**Tracey** (*sensing a chill in the air*) What's up with you? Not giving me my morning shag? Where's the old broomstick in the back this morning? Am I not putting the lead in your pencil anymore?

**David** Look, I've been thinking. I just don't feel that I love you anymore.

*Tracey freaks out.*

**Tracey** What do you mean? I thought we were sorted, sorted for life. We've been living together for four years and everything. What about the kid? What about Chardonnay?

**David** *(heavy sigh)* When I met you, I thought you were the love of my life. My oh-how-clichéd 'soul-mate'. What I neglected to tell you was that I was taking the world's most effective anti-depressant, Clomipramine. Now that I've stopped it, I can see how much it was messing with my head. It's not that life with you was peachy. It was the bloody pills I'd been taking. You can't even trust your own emotions these days. Everything just boils down to whatever chemicals you've consumed. Clomipramine made me see the world through rose-tinted lenses, but that's not the *real* world, that's just an alteration of brain chemicals, that's not seeing the *real* situation. The *real* situation is that I'm stuck with a woman, a *girl*, half my age, supporting both her and her child without any real social life. I don't even get time to see my old mates anymore.

*Tracey looks thrown. David's threatening to take away her security and her stability. Tracey tries to hang onto the relationship.*

**Tracey** Look, how do you know that coming off the anti-depressants hasn't thrown you into a depression? Maybe you're blaming everything on your life situation and our relationship. Maybe it's just an imbalance in brain chemicals that the Clomipramine was correcting. You should go back on the drugs. How suddenly did you come off them anyway?

**David** Just last week. Stopped cold turkey.

**Tracey** You idiot! You should never stop anti-depressants without seeing your doctor.

**David** My GP's just a quack, doesn't know his arse from his elbow. I feel trapped, claustrophobic. I want my freedom back.

**Tracey** Well, what about me and Chardonnay? Where do we stand in all this?

**David** You'll be all right. There's still a spare room at your mother's, isn't there?

*Tracey becomes really angry, smashes a table lamp over his head.*

**David** Look, calm down, calm down, take a deep breath.

**Tracey** *(totally loses it)* Don't patronise me, you stupid prick. Cripes, you harden yourself to get by in a hard, cold world. Then you meet somebody who you think is special, the one for you – somebody you think can take care of you and your child. You let down your guard an inch, let them in and all they do is screw you over in the end. You're better off alone.

*David looks down at his hands, silent.*

**Tracey** *(hard and cold)* Fine, listen, I'm not gonna be sticking around where I'm not wanted.

*Packs her meagre possessions into a bag. Takes the baby from the cot.*

**Tracey** *(to baby)* Come on, Chardonnay, let's bust this joint. Back to Mum's it is. *(Over shoulder to David, venomously.)* Probably see you around some time. Don't bother getting up. I'll just do my own thing.

# SCENE TWENTY-TWO

*The Screen reads 28 February 2035 at 19:52:35.*

*Posh bar.*

*Isobella is sitting at a bar guzzling wine in Tracey-style manner. Tarquin enters talking on phone. Throughout this scene Isobella shifts between Isobella-mode and Tracey-mode.*

**Tarquin** Oh hello darling. Sorry I'm late. I've just been shopping for a new iPhone. The very latest thing.

*Starts showing her the functionality. Isobella (in Tracey mode) pours herself another glass of wine, guzzles it.*

**Tarquin** Easy on the wine, old thing. Had a rough day?

**Isobella** *(in Tracey mode)* Yeah, bloody awful.

**Tarquin** Foul language? From my immaculately-mannered Isobella? Whatever's gotten into you?

**Isobella** *(in Isobella mode)* Gosh, I really don't know. Every now and then I have these interludes where somebody else's words come out of my mouth.

**Tarquin** It must be the segment, darling. There's quite simply no other explanation.

**Isobella** Yes, we really ought to start training it up.

## SCENE TWENTY-THREE

*The Screen reads 7 March 2035 at 07:45:15.*

*Isobella and Tarquin's apartment.*

*Isobella and Tarquin waking up in bed together, echoes of David and Tracey.*

**Isobella** You're a bit frosty this morning, darling. No peck on the cheek?

*Holds out cheek for a peck.*

**Tarquin** Listen. I've been thinking. I think it's time for us to go our separate ways.

**Isobella** *(alarmed)* What do you mean? You said that you loved me.

**Tarquin** Yes, but that was before the implant. You're not *you* anymore. You've been *invaded*. Taken over.

**Isobella** I can't *help* it. I can't control my inner chav. The segment's got its own mind.

**Tarquin** I can't share my life with a woman who is one person one minute and a different person the next.

**Isobella** *(defensive)* Fine, be that way then.

**Tarquin** Well, let's see how things pan out.

# SCENE TWENTY-FOUR

*The Screen reads 7 March 2035 at 10:50:30.*

*Isobella and Tarquin's apartment.*

**Isobella** I don't know if my body was rejecting the implant, despite the anti-rejection drug, Cyclosporine, that I was taking, but four years after the implant I hit a really bad patch. Couldn't leave the house. Started freaking out in supermarkets. There was so much bloody *choice*. Did I want green olives or black? Did I need arborio rice or basmati? Hovis bread or Sunblest? And then there were all the other people. Women with screaming brats orbiting the trolleys. Men who helpfully park their trolleys sideways in the aisle. I went to the physician and he prescribed an anti-depressant, but it didn't make much difference. It was as if I was suddenly lacking a protective coating. The wall which, in a normal person, keeps the inside in and the outside out had disintegrated. I was the walking wounded. A slab of scar issue. I took to ordering my groceries online. I downloaded my books directly from the library onto my Kobo. For weeks I was too scared to leave the house.

**Tarquin** *(head in hands)* I just can't take this anymore. Where's my little princess gone? Right, we're taking you to the hospital.

**Isobella** I'm not going into a psychiatric institution.

**Tarquin** It's the safest place for you.

**Isobella** I refuse.

*Runs offstage*

## SCENE TWENTY-FIVE

*The Screen reads 12 April 2035 at 11:15:25.*

*Isobella and Tarquin's apartment.*

*Tarquin enters all jolly, but with a false ring to it.*

**Tarquin** I know what'll rekindle the spark in our relationship. A weekend away at the country lodge.

**Isobella** Could we really go there?

**Tarquin** Sure. Why don't you pack a few things. (*Phones*) Taxi?

*Puts bags in taxi. Takes her to a psychiatric hospital.*

**Isobella** Hey, what's going on? This isn't the country lodge. This looks like a hospital.

*Tarquin says nothing, just takes Isobella by the hand and walks her into the hospital.*


## SCENE TWENTY-SIX

*The Screen reads 30 April 2035 at 16:52:53.*

*Psychiatric hospital.*

*Isobella is lying in bed. Tracey enters. Tracey is allocated as nurse and is in uniform.*

**Tracey** (*surprised*) Bloody hell! What are you doing here then? You seemed right jolly when we left the hospital four years ago.

**Isobella** Tarquin dumped me after the brain implant started making me have a split personality.

**Tracey** It must have been quite frightening for him. Sort of demonic possession?

**Isobella** I don't believe in that rubbish. It was my brain struggling to cope with the segment. At the risk of sounding like a psychology textbook, it put too much of a strain on our relationship. My eyes were opened. I realised that I was just his little trophy – valued for my exterior rather than my interior. Once a piece of *you* was inserted into my frontal lobe, the gloss wore off and I was no longer his great catch, his trendy little accessory. The best part is that he got me admitted by using a trick. Pretended that he was taking me away for a weekend in the country. We got a taxi and everything. Then he dumped me here at this psychiatric hospital.

**Tracey** Cripes, what an *arsehole!*

**Isobella** Yes, very T.S. Eliot of him. Shoving his partner in a psychiatric institution when the shit hits the fan and leaving her there.

**Tracey** Ain't it funny? I've had a similar experience myself. Moved in with the man who I thought was the love of my life, who encouraged me to achieve my goals, supported me through my nursing training. The minute we move in together, he wants to be single again.

**Isobella** Crikey, what a loser. What a wimp.

**Tracey** Yeah, well, turns out it wasn't love after all. He was taking some sort of uber anti-depressant, so when he met me he may as well have been on E. All loved up. Once the high wore off and he was on a comedown, the love evaporated. It wasn't 'love' actually. Our entire relationship was based on a chemical high masquerading as a permanent Valentine's Day. Just a chemical reaction in his brain.

**Isobella** Bloody hell! Modern life, eh?

**Tracey** Yeah, tell me about it, man. You'd be surprised and amazed at the patients we admit here. Half of the city's been through these doors. Hey, listen – what do you think would happen if part of *your* brain got implanted in my frontal lobe? Would I be invaded by a portion of posh?

**Isobella** Hey, that's a thought. But why are you in here then? Not having any repercussions from the surgery, are you?

**Tracey** I work here, innit. It's my job. I'm your allocated nurse, love.

**Isobella** Oh, it'll be like old times. Remember that time in hospital?

**Tracey** Yeah that were a hoot, weren't it? How could I forget? Seems like we got a lot in common despite our class differences. It's not *your* fault you were born with the silver spoon, anymore than it was *my* fault I was born with the plastic spoon.

*Hands Isobella a handful of pills.*

**Tracey** Here we are then. Here's your night-time meds. We hand out pills like candy here. I have mixed emotions about this. On the one hand, if somebody is genuinely having a psychiatric emergency then medication can be a plaster cast around a damaged mind. On the other hand, do I really believe in chemical lobotomies? Isn't a nervous breakdown just a sane response to a planet gone completely berserk?

**Isobella** I hear what you're saying. Maybe Howard Hughes had the right idea after all, locking himself up and drinking his own urine. A suitable last resort when it all just gets too much. Fiscal cliffs, corporate corruption, bad guys posing as good guys, global warming, twenty-six per cent unemployment in Greece and Spain, the American credit crunch, information overload – the endless bombardment of messages, from newspapers, magazines, pamphlets, train stations, the limitless amount of junk that is to be found on the internet. My goodness, I think if aliens came to earth they might remark that the internet was the dominant organism and the humans were merely its servants.

**Tracey** Listen. Since the men in our lives have turned out to be such swine, maybe we could make a go of it together.

**Isobella** Sure. Why not? Everybody needs a hand to hold. Part of you is already in me anyway.

**Tracey** Together in body and mind. Here's to our future together.

*Kiss each other both sides of cheek – i.e. the Euro-kiss.*

**Isobella** Hey, what do you think about donating our brains to the London Museum of Natural History? After all, we are pioneers of a sort.

**Tracey** More like freaks, lab exhibits.

**Isobella** Do you think that the heart rules the brain or the brain rules the heart?

**Tracey** How the heck should I know? That one's been puzzling humankind since the dawn of time, innit?

*Whips out a hipflask and two shot-glasses from bum-bag. Pours them both a shot.*

**Tracey** Listen. I'm not normally allowed to drink on the job, but let's share a quick whiskey.

**Isobella** Cheers. Here's to our future health and happiness.

*The two women share a whiskey. The main stage darkens.*

*The clock disappears from The Screen. The Screen displays two brains at the top and two hearts underneath. Stays this way for 20-30 seconds and then changes so that the hearts are on top.*

**Other books by Laura Solomon**

**published by Proverse Hong Kong**

*Frida Kahlo's Cry* (2015).

*University Days* (2014). (Sequel to *Instant Messages*)

*In Vitro* (poetry collection), first published by HeadworX (Wellington, New Zealand), 2011. (2014)

*Vera Magpie* (novella) (2013).

*An Imitation of Life*, second revised enlarged edition (novel) (2013).

*The Shingle Bar Sea Monster and Other Stories* (2012).

*Hilary and David* (epistolary novel) (2011). A Proverse Prize Publication.

*Instant Messages* (novella) (2010). Winner of the inaugural Proverse Prize (2009).

# FIND OUT MORE ABOUT PROVERSE AUTHORS, BOOKS, EVENTS, AND INTERNATIONAL LITERARY PRIZES

**Visit our website**
http://www.proversepublishing.com

**Visit our distributor's website**
<www.chineseupress.com>

**Follow us on Twitter**
Follow news and conversation: <twitter.com/Proversebooks>
*OR*
Copy and paste the following to your browser window and follow the instructions: https://twitter.com/#!/ProverseBooks

**"Like" us on www.facebook.com/ProversePress**

**Request our E-Newsletter**
Send your request to info@proversepublishing.com.

**Availability**
Most titles are available in Hong Kong and world-wide from our Hong Kong-based Distributor,
The Chinese University Press of Hong Kong,
The Chinese University of Hong Kong, Shatin, NT, Hong Kong SAR, China. Web: chineseupress.com

All titles are available from Proverse Hong Kong and the Proverse Hong Kong UK-based Distributor.

We have stock-holding retailers in Hong Kong, Singapore (Select Books), Canada (Elizabeth Campbell Books), Principality of Andorra (Llibreria La Puça, La Llibreria).

Orders can be made from bookshops in the UK and elsewhere.

**Ebooks**
Most of our titles are available also as Ebooks.

www.ingramcontent.com/pod-product-compliance
Lightning Source LLC
Chambersburg PA
CBHW051134160426
**43195CB00014B/2467**